Angel Romero: In Concert

by Angel Romero

1 2

Visit us on the Web at www.melbay.com — E-mail us at email@melbay.com

Table of Contents

*I would like to give thanks to my dear friend and very fine guitarist, Robert Wetzel for spending many hours
assisting me in transferring all of my fingerings for this edition due to my very heavy schedule.
I would also like to thank my dearest wife, Nefretiri,
for spending countless hours assisting in the full process of this book.
I would like to dedicate this publication to my twelve year old beloved daughter Isabella
who sat along side me and gave me inspiration throughout my work.*

Angel Romero

Introduction

With this publication, I bring to guitarists throughout the world the programming force and substance of my concerts. To me, performing a concert is a kind of un-natural situation so I must have an emotional tool that makes me forget anything but the music. And in so doing, I try to bring as much of a positive force to the stage as possible.

In this collection I combine some of the greatest composers that we have available to us who have also given me joy throughout my career. The glorious and sacred Fourth Lute Suite of J.S. Bach begins my concert journey, not only emotionally, but also technically. Then I move on to a different interpretive emotion with the prolific and deep compositions of Domenico Scarlatti. As a matter of fact, Scarlatti was the composer I played in my first concert at age five.

My musical palette also has extended to the great French composers: Debussy and Satie; they represent my love for the French Impressionist such as Monet, Renoir and Degas. These selections achieve the same atmosphere and exhibit a full representation of these masters' brushstrokes.

In the second half of my concerts I turn to what I call my "inner free spirit," since these pieces represent the time in which I reach into my roots as a Spaniard. These pieces are left for the second half because all boundaries within me cease to exist. Being the music of my country, I find these pieces to be the easiest way to express myself without any of the academic considerations of music.

I hope that this collection brings you the same joy and spiritual uplifting experience as it has for me throughout my career.

With warmest wishes for your success,
Angel Romero

Lautensuite Nr. 4 E-Dur

Bach-Werkverzeichnis 1006 A

Präludium

arr. © Angel Romero. All Rights Reserved. Used by Permission.

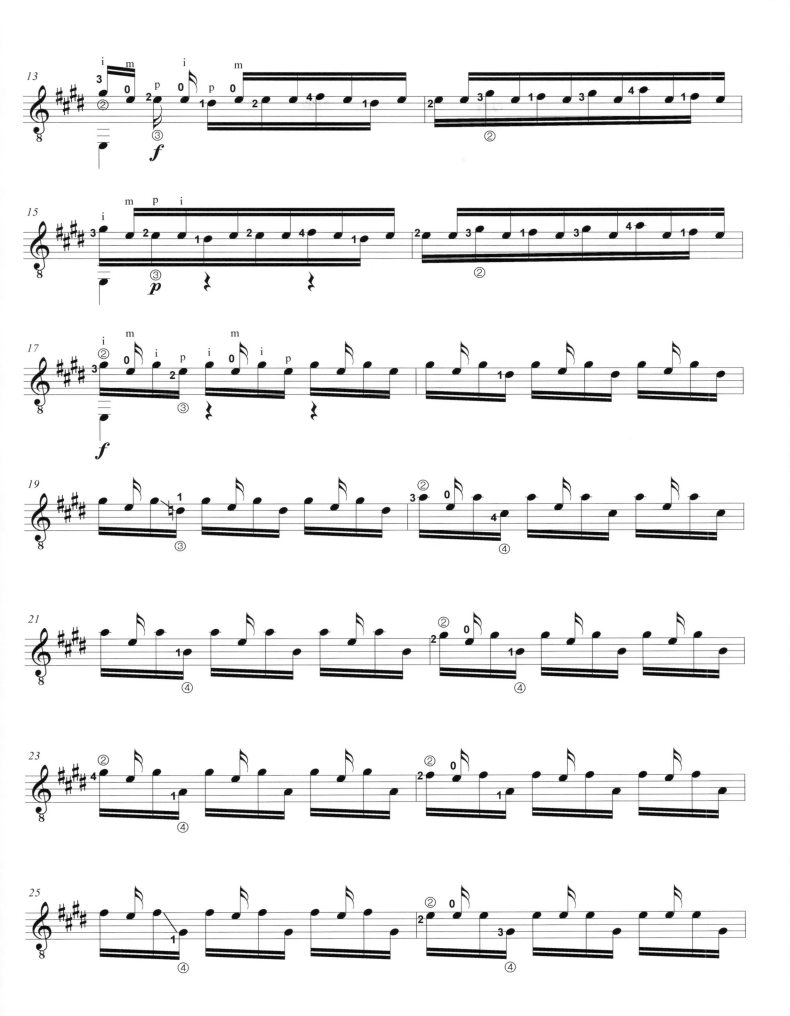

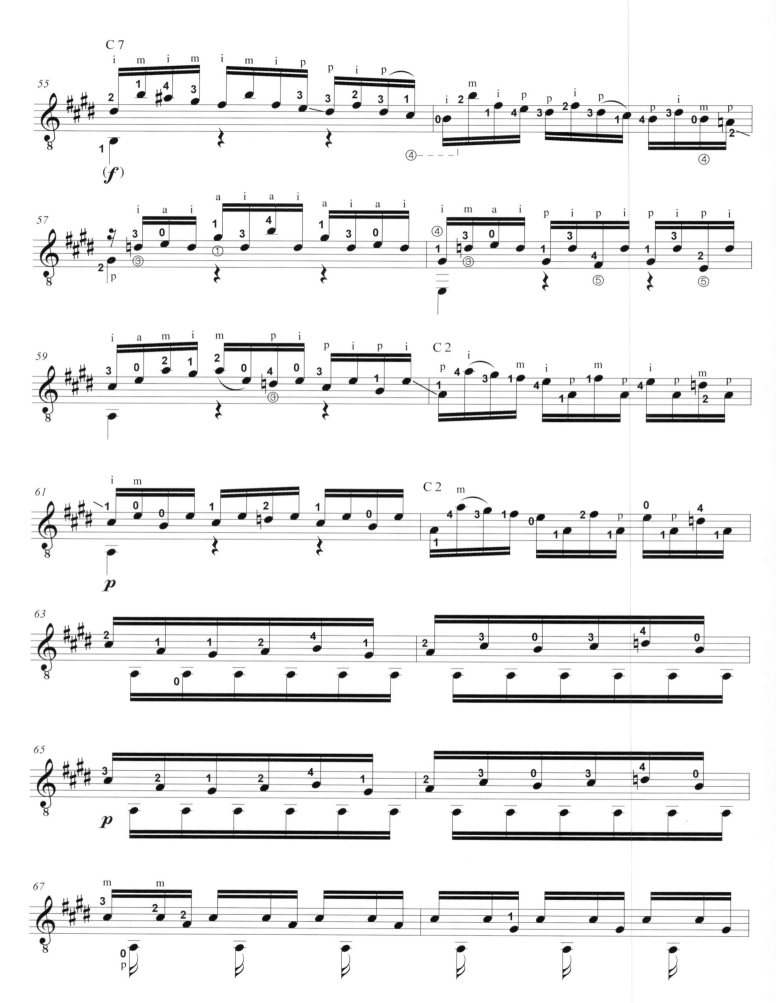

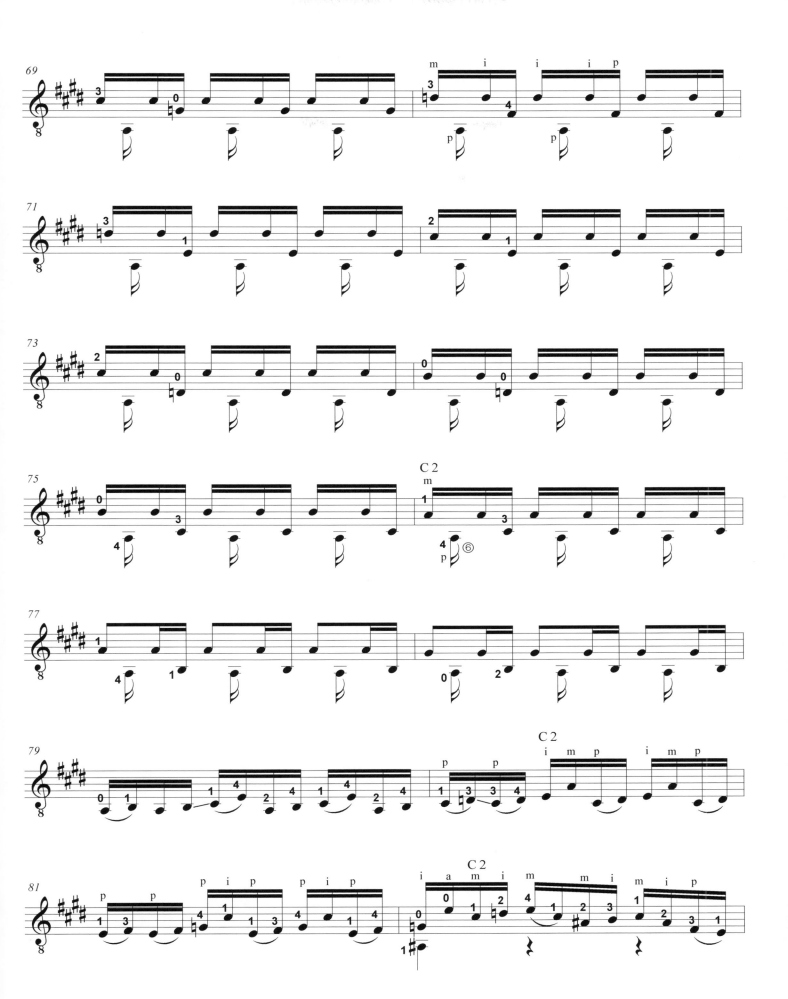

10

Loure

14

Gavotte en Rondeau

18

Menuett 1

21

Menuett 2

arr. © Angel Romero. All Rights Reserved. Used by Permission.

23

Bourrée

Gigue

27

Sonata, K. 213

Domenico Scarlatti
(1685-1757)

* A with appoggiatura

Clair de Lune

from "Suite Bergamasque"

bar with 1st finger
4 & 5 strings

XII

(All thumb strum)

36

Gymnopedie

Erik Satie

bring down first finger to cover both ⑥ & ⑤

Tango

Francisco Tarrega

Rumores de la Caleta

Isaac Albeniz

Sevilla

(Sevillanas)
(Suite española, No. 3)

Isaac Albeniz

Tempo I

D. S. (from 𝄋 to 𝄌 m. 2-23, then to m. 51 on page 48)

47

D. S. (from 𝄋 to 𝄌 m. 2-23, then to Coda on page 50)